The Little Book of
Brilliant Quotes

Heather Jane-James © 2018

www.heatherjanejames.com

ISBN 9781728750743

2

AUTHOR'S NOTE:

This book is factually accurate to the best of the author's knowledge. It is not however anything more than a representation of the author's knowledge, therefore rather than facts information offered should be viewed as the author's opinion not as an expert or historical statement of record. The notes are provided for two reasons. Firstly because the book is about quotes, therefore other people's words, the author could not hold copyright unless she herself had written the majority of the text, which she has. Quotes actually form less than 10% of the words used. Secondly selecting the quotes for this book and the information provided about their sources was, for the author, the real joy of putting this together!

Hopefully it's inspiring, interesting and sparks curiosity!

3

"Once you choose hope, anything is possible"

CHRISTOPHER REEVE

b.25 September 1952, New York City, New York, USA
d. 10 October 2004, Mount Kisco, New York, USA

Best Known For:

Playing *Superman* alias Clark Kent in the films of the same name made during the 1970s and 1980s.
In 1995 Reeve was left completely paralysed from the neck down after being thrown from his horse. After his accident he set up the Christopher Reeve foundation, and despite always needing a ventilator and being in a wheelchair was a prolific campaigner and fundraiser for spinal cord injury research.

"I believe that everything happens for a reason. People change so that you can learn to let go, things go wrong so that you appreciate them when they're right, you believe lies so you eventually learn to trust no one but yourself, and sometimes good things fall apart so better things can fall together"

MARILYN MONROE

b.1 June 1926, Los Angeles, California, USA
d.5 August 1962, Brentwood, California, USA

Best Known For:

Being one of 20th Century's "golden age of Hollywood" superstars and the world's first and arguably greatest sex symbol. Monroe was a model and actress, and became a glamour icon for not just the era but for generations to this day. She was relentlessly pursued by the press who placed her private life under constant scrutiny and invasion so that her lovers, mental health and sexuality were always being speculated upon. She died at only 36 years old, which seems incomprehensible given her films turned over what would be $2bn in today's money. Born Norma Jeane Mortenson she was known as Norma Jean Baker from the age of 15 when her mother remarried, and although was frequently in foster care throughout her childhood she fought hard to study acting having decide that's what she wanted to do at the age of 5 (Monroe was her mother's maiden name). She had 3 marriages, two to equally prolific men of the era - the New York Yankees baseball star Joe DiMaggio and the renowned playwright Arthur Miller. Affairs between Monroe and then US President John F Kennedy and his brother, Robert Kennedy, the then US Attorney General were strongly rumoured to this day to have played a part in her untimely death from a drugs overdose.

"Happiness is when what you think, what you say, and what you do are in harmony"

MAHATMA GANDHI

b. 22 October 1869, Porbandar, India
d. 30 January 1948, New Delhi, India

Best Known For:

Leading India to independence from British Rule in 1947 (after a struggle that started in 1915), for being the leading global advocate of nonviolent change and peaceful demonstration. A huge and far reaching permanent influence on both East and West with regard to nation states, politics, justice, civil rights, humanitarian relief, spirituality, leadership, world peace and poverty - to name a few - means it's rather difficult to provide an adequate synopsis! Mohandas Karamchand Gandhi was born into a large family, the youngest son of his father's fourth wife, he had 3 sisters and two brothers. His mother was a devout follower of Vaishnavism and Jainism so principles such as ahimsa (that harm to one living thing is harm to all), fasting, vegetarianism and morality were the normal values of his life. Having said that Gandhi, so called Mahatma because it means "Great Soul", was not always so virtuous - he was not particularly academic, a move to London where he trained at the Inner Temple to become a barrister following funding from his brother was given on Gandhi's promise to steer clear of women, meat and alcohol! From London he started his journey into human rights and social activism, heading first to South Africa then back to his homeland where he became leader of the Indian National Congress in 1920. Despite achieving the successful return of India to self-rule, and whilst Gandhi believed in religious pluralism and freedom, not all his compatriots were as inclusive and ultimately the British India Empire was partitioned into 2 states: India which was mainly Hindu and Pakistan which was principally Muslim. With the partition followed mass movement of different groups,and religious war and chaos ensued. Gandhi continued to plead for peace regularly fasting and touring both India and Pakistan as they struggled to readjust. He was assassinated by a Hindu extremist.

"Be the change you wish to see in the world"

"I will not let anyone walk through my mind with their dirty feet"

"Where there is love, there is life"

"Not all who wander are lost"

J R R TOLKIEN

b. 3 January 1892, Bloemfontein, South Africa
d. 2 September 1973, Bournemouth, Dorset UK

Best Known For:

The Lord of the Rings. John Ronald Reuel Tolkien was born in South Africa whilst his British parents were stationed there, holidaying in England when he was three, his father suddenly died and the family decided to stay in the UK. Brought up in the Midlands, Tolkien was a bright child who could read and write by the age of 4. His early reading life was driven by the work of Scottish poet George Macdonald - who is also cited as mentor to other famed writes such as CS Lewis and WH Auden. Often inventing his own languages with friends and cousins in his youth, Tolkien followed an academic path, interspersed by service in both World Wars, the second as a cryptographer. He was a highly respected philologist, studying and teaching at Oxford. Other works include The Hobbit and posthumously published The Silmarillion. Lord of the Rings was released in 3 parts from 1954-55, has been translated into over 50 languages, sold more than 150 million copies and the franchise including movies and games is currently estimated at $5.82billion!

"And now here is my secret, a very simple secret: It is only with the heart that one can see rightly; what is essential is invisible to the eye"

ANTOINE DE SAINT-EXUPÉRY

b. 9 June 1900, Lyon, France
d. 31 July 1944, Marseille, France

Best Known For:

The Little Prince. Antoine Marie Jean-Baptiste Roger, comte de Saint-Exupéry, apart from having one helluva name was a pilot, journalist, poet and writer. That most famous work has been translated into 300 languages and is still one of the best selling children's books in the world today. He was reported Missing In Action close to the end of World War II flying as part of the Free French Air Force. Although firstly staying in France following the France-Germany Armistice in 1940, he spent the two years prior to his death in the USA, using his status as a philanthropic influencer following his 1939 work *Terre des hommes—Man and His World* to raise awareness of the Nazi bloodshed across Europe. *Terre des hommes* is still revered and utilised by humanitarian groups worldwide.

"A wise man can learn more from a foolish question than a fool can learn from a wise answer"

BRUCE LEE

b. 27 November 1940, Chinatown, San Francisco, USA
d. 30 July 1973, Kowloon Tong, Hong Kong

Best Known For:

Being a general martial arts legend, a film icon of the 20th century, and widely credited with bringing martial arts into mainstream awareness and worldwide recognition. Born *Lee Jun-fan* (李振藩) in San Francisco whilst his parents were on tour (his father was a famous Cantonese opera singer, his mother part of the mixed race lineage of the "grand old man of Hong Kong" Sir Robert Hotung), Lee was only there as a baby. He grew up in Kowloon. Returning to the US in early adulthood to study, amongst other things, philosophy, he also began teaching martial arts, later developing his own schools and accepted forms of kung fu. His most famous films included *The Big Boss* (1971), *Fist of Fury* (1972) and *Way of the Dragon* (1972). He died aged 32 of a cerebral enema, having been taken to hospital whilst filming.

"Your task is not to seek for love, but merely to seek and find all the barriers within yourself that you have built against it"

RUMI

b. 30 September 1207, Balkha, Afghanistan
d. 17 December 1273 Konya, Turkey

Best Known For:

His words and spiritual wisdom. Jalāl ad-Dīn Muhammad Rūmī became one of the world's most prolific Sufis - the branch of Islamic mysticism that began circa 10th Century AD. Nicknamed "The Bird" Rumi roamed towns and villages across Persia - the huge area of the Middle East that spread from Turkey, Iran and Syria into Egypt and the Emirates in the south and Pakistan and China to the East. Facts pertaining to Rumi's life are difficult to definitively establish, records say that he produced 30,000 poems, others 90,000. Whichever its volume is not small. Rumi has increased in popularity greatly with the advent of social media - the lines and verses he created forming the basis of millions of posts. From a wealthy background Rumi befriended a travelling mystic known as Shams, from whom he learnt that connection with God was open to all mankind. He is the founder of the Mevlevi, famed for the Whirling Dervishes.

"Start by doing what's necessary; then do what's possible; and suddenly you are doing the impossible"

ST FRANCIS OF ASSISI

b. 1181 or 1182, Assisi, Italy
d. 3 October 1226, Assisi, Italy

Best Known For:

Talking to the animals, amongst other things. St Francis was a Christian mystic, monk and preacher who founded numerous orders within the Catholic Church. Giovanni di Pietro di Bernardone was nicknamed "Francis" by his father, an Italian, due to his son's obsession with all things French, including splendid clothes and possessions no doubt influenced by his French aristocratic mother. In his late teens and early twenties Francis had numerous spiritual experiences and whilst he briefly flirted with a return to French finery at the age of 23 he renounced the material world completely and set about devoting his life to the love and service of God and others. He believed strongly in the sanctity of all living things, and was canonised only two years after his death. He is the patron saint of Italy and animals.

"Darkness cannot drive out darkness; only light can do that. Hate cannot drive out hate; only love can do that"

"Every man must decide whether he will walk in the light of creative altruism or in the darkness of destructive selfishness"

"He who is devoid of the power to forgive is devoid of the power to love"

MARTIN LUTHER KING JR

b. 5 January 1929, Atlanta, Georgia, USA
d. 4 April 1968, Memphis, Tennessee, USA

Best Known For:

Civil Rights, racial equality, peaceful protest, human rights, removing racial segregation in North America, setting the bar for peaceful revolution, civil disobedience and nonviolent protest across the globe, inspiring millions, the world's most quoted rallying speech beginning, "I have a dream…"

When Reverend Martin Luther King Sr. and Alberta Williams King welcomed their second child, Michael, little could they have imagined his future. Assassinated at the age of only 39 he left his widow Coretta, 4 children and a legacy of equal opportunities legislation in the USA and a global influence on fair treatment for all human beings. A bright child he attended school under scholarship, gained his first degree, a Bachelors in Sociology by 19, and despite well documented intellectual struggles with the technical veracity of the Bible had become a preacher at this age too. He ultimately went on to gain a Ph.D in Systematic Theology from Boston. One of the key leaders of the Montgomery Bus Boycotts in 1955 he became famed as a civil rights activist and spokesperson for the movement. The boycotts lead to the decision of the US Supreme Court in Bowder v Gayle, a case he was involved in bringing - Aurelia Bowder being the lead plaintiff of 5 black women who had refused the give up their seat on a bus to a white (the case of Rosa Parks - one of the most famous seat keepers - was already tied up in lower courts. Bowder was the second woman to be prosecuted and fined a month after the first, 15 year old Claudette Colwin, some 8 months before the Parks' case catapulted the issue into the media spotlight). The case removed segregation on transport, schools and public offices. During this time his home was bombed, and he founded the Southern Christian Leadership Conference to direct and garner support for nonviolent protest against racial segregation. In 1957 he lead the first of his marches to Washington, the Prayer Pilgrimage, although the more well known is the 1963 march from where his "I have a dream" speech was made. Only six days after his death the Civil Rights (Fair Housing) Act of 1968 was passed under Lyndon Johnson, where rights were established not just to prevent racism but also sexism and income based discrimination. As well as the victory in Bowder vs Gayle (Gayle was the Mayor of Montgomery, Alabama) in his lifetime Dr King saw the introduction of the Civil Rights Act of 1964 and the Voting Rights Act of 1965. He was the youngest ever awarded recipient of the Nobel Peace Prize until Malala Yousafzai in 2014.

"Only in the darkness can you see the stars"

"In the end, we will remember not the words of our enemies, but the silence of our friends"

"Injustice anywhere is a threat to justice everywhere"

"It takes courage to grow up and be who you really are"

EE CUMMINGS

"Be yourself, everyone else is taken"

OSCAR WILDE

"To thine own self be true"

WILLIAM SHAKESPEARE

"Beauty begins the moment you decide to be yourself"

COCO CHANEL

"And those who were seen dancing were thought to be insane by those who could not hear the music"

FRIEDRICH NIETZSCHE

b. 15 October 1844, Rocken, Prussia, German Federation
d. 25 August 1900, Weimar, Saxe-Weimar-Eisenach, German Empire

Best Known For:

People arguing over how to pronounce his name, it is "Knee-cher" to rhyme with beacher, and being a profound philosopher, writer, composer, poet and philologist. In 1869 he became Chair of Classical Philosophy at Basel University, one of the youngest ever at any institution in the world. Nietzsche suffered with his physical and mental health his entire life, flitting between travelling with other creatives and intellectuals such as the composer Robert Wagner, the Swiss feminist Meta von Salis, philosophers Paul Ree and Lou Salome and being cared for by his mother and sister. Self medicating was a persistent hobby and he is believed to have been addicted to various opiates and hallucinogens for much of his life. He produced works quite manically, some huge pieces in less than a fortnight, nearly 20 were published between 1872 and his mental breakdown in 1889. On announcing "God is Dead" he caused uproar to many religions, however he himself never argued against divinity, moreover that man did a poor job with it.

"And now that you don't have to be perfect, you can be good"

JOHN STEINBECK

b. 27 February 1902, Salinas, California, USA
d. 20 December 1968, New York City, USA

Best Known For:

Authoring *The Grapes of Wrath*, which won him a Pulitzer Prize in 1939 and was made into a multi Academy Award winning film starring Henry Fonda in 1940. A straightforward middle class upbringing became littered with chance experiences and encounters that would later shape much of his work, which dealt with the dark side of reality as much as the positive. Although he had earned a place at Stanford University to study English Literature he never graduated, and moved back and forth between the East and West Coasts in a bid to get his work published and recognised. Most of his life he spent in California however and much of his works are based there. Married twice with two children he authored some 27 works in his lifetime and was awarded the Nobel Prize for Literature in 1962. Steinbeck is considered one of the US' literary legends, *The Grapes of Wrath* sits alongside other well known greats such as *Of Mice and Men, East of Eden* and *Tortilla Flat*.

"It is the mark of an educated mind to be able to entertain a thought without accepting it"

ARISTOTLE

b.384 BC, Stagira, Macedonia
d. 322 BC, Chalcis, Greece

Best Known For:

Being one of the Greek Philosophy Daddies, basically. He is the most celebrated student of Plato, who created the world's first ever institution designed solely for the pursuit of academic, intellectual and spiritual betterment in 387 B.C. Aristotle attended Plato's Academy for 20 years, before he left to create his own school at The Lyceum in Athens having been invited there to tutor to the future king, who would become Alexander the Great. At least two thirds of Aristotle's work is considered missing, which is astounding given the volume that remains on topics as far reaching as astronomy, the soul, metaphysics, botany, physics, mathematics, ethics, religion, evolution and logic. Many of Aristotle's theories and musings seemed beyond the realms of what we believed to be possible in the time period, notably on subjects such as the solar system and metaphysics, however have since been proven as correct today.

"Character cannot be developed in ease and quiet. Only through experience of trial and suffering can the soul be strengthened, ambition inspired, and success achieved"

HELEN KELLER

b. 27 June 1880, Tuscumbia, Alabama, USA
d. 1 June 1968, Easton, Connecticut, USA

Best Known For:

Being the first deaf and blind person to graduate at degree level and being at the forefront of early 20th Century Civil Rights movements. Left deaf and bling by a mystery illness she was seen by teacher of the deaf Alexander Graham Bell - more famous as the inventor of the telephone - when she was six years old. He introduced Keller to Anne Sullivan, who was Keller's teacher and companion her whole life. Keller not only learnt to communicate but went on to write 12 books including *The Miracle Worker* and *The World I Live In*, and over 500 essays, journalistic articles and latterly speeches (read by interpreters) not just on disabilities but women's rights and workforce equality. Lyndon Johnson awarded Keller the Presidential Medal of Freedom in 1964.

"If you never change your mind, why have one?"

EDWARD DE BONO

b. 19 May 1933, St Julian's Bay, Malta

Best Known For:

Lateral Thinking. He coined the phrase, wrote the book and gave the world the Six Thinking Hats - a methodology of examining a problem from different perspectives employed by corporations and governments alike. Born in Malta De Bono is the son of a doctor and journalist. He graduated with his first degree in medicine at only 15 years old. He was a recipient of the men only Rhodes Scholarship to study at Oxford University, another famous beneficiary being former US President Bill Clinton. There he gained a masters in psychology and physiology, which he followed with various doctorates in medicine and design. He is still a professor at universities in Malta, Birmingham, Pretoria, Dublin and Arizona, having also taught at Oxford, Cambridge and Harvard. He has written over 80 books translated into over 40 languages on creative thinking and problem solving.

"Everyone should have their mind blown once a day"

NEIL DEGRASSE TYSON

b. 5 October 1958, Manhattan, New York, USA

Best Known For:

Being a scientist that people relate to. DeGrasse Tyson's popular works on everything astrophysics include *Merlin's Tour of the Universe*, *Just Visiting the Planet*, *Death by Black Hole* and *Astrophysics for People in a Hurry*. He is a director of the Hayden Planetarium in New York, part of the American Natural History Museum. He received NASA's award for distinguished public service in 2004 and has presented numerous television series and documentaries on the nature of the universe. Born to humanitarian focused parents in the Bronx, schooled at the Bronx High School for Science, he was giving talks and writing articles on space from the age of 15. Although he attended Harvard to study for his bachelor's degree in Physics he was invited first by another Ivy League university, Cornell, which he declined!

"Most of us were taught that God would love us if and when we change. In fact, God loves you so that you can change. What empowers change, what makes you desirous of change is the experience of love. It is that inherent experience of love that becomes the engine of change"

RICHARD ROHR

b. 20 March 1943, Topeka, Kansas, USA

Best Known For:

Being the priest who people relate to. A prolific writer having published over 100 books on Christianity, Prayer, Meditation and Spirituality he runs the Centre for Action and Contemplation in New Mexico. Always destined for great things he recalls "bumping into" Mother Teresa and Thomas Merton, together, as a young man.

"It's something my mother believed in: If you are in a position of privilege, if you can put your name to something that you genuinely believe in, you can smash any stigma you want, and you can encourage anybody to do anything"

HRH PRINCE HENRY of WALES, DUKE of SUSSEX

b. 15 September 1984, St Mary's Hospital, London, UK

Best Known For:

Being the younger son of HRH Prince Charles, next in line to the British throne and Diana, Princess of Wales. The world has watched the boy who walked behind his mother's coffin in front of a worldwide audience of 2.5billion turn into a serviceman for his country, generate an impressive charitable presence in Africa and create the Invictus Games. Recently married to American actress Meghan Markle they are expecting their first child in 2019.

"I don't trust people who don't love themselves and tell me, 'I love you.' ... There is an African saying which is: Be careful when a naked person offers you a shirt"

MAYA ANGELOU

b. 4 April 1928, St. Louis, Missouri, USA
d. 28 May 2014, Winston-Salem, North Carolina, USA

Best Known For:

Brilliant poetry, Civil Rights and writing *I Know Why the Caged Bird Sings*, the first of seven autobiographical novels that describe what it was like growing up and being a part of society as an African American woman in her lifetime. She worked alongside Martin Luther King Jr as a coordinator for activist demonstrations. Her early childhood was safeguarded in the care of her wealthy grandmother. At the age of 8 she stopped speaking after being raped and abused by her mother's boyfriend. Although she returned to her grandmother she did not find her voice for another five years, during which time she existed in books, silent reflection on her internal, spiritual world and observation of the detail of her external one. This would, when she began to communicate, give her words great depth and meaning - she has received many literary awards and the Presidential Medal of Freedom in 2011.

"Once you make a decision, the universe conspires to make it happen"

RALPH WALDO EMERSON

b. 5 May 1803, Boston, Massachusetts, USA
d. 27 April 1882, Concord, Massachusetts, USA

Best Known For:

Being part of the transcendentalism movement of the early 19th Century and his works on philosophy, psychology and spirituality, many of which are still studied and used in therapy and motivation today. Transcendentalism merged both East and West religious ideals and was based in the principle of inherent good in all. He is credited with guiding a huge sway of later philosophers including Henry David Thoreau, Walt Whitman and Friedrich Nietzsche. A bright child he was raised mainly by the women in his family after the death of his father when he was 8. By the age of 14 he was at Harvard studying theology. Initially a clergyman he totally re-thought his relationship to church teachings after losing his first wife to tuberculosis at the age of 27. He travelled widely teaching on pantheism, spiritual experiences and connection with one's own soul, he also set up schools for teaching women and arguing for the abolition of slavery, which were revolutionary for the time. Six of his books, which are more akin to collections of essays, are still in print today.

"The fight is won or lost far away from witnesses - behind the lines, in the gym, and out there on the road, long before I dance under those lights"

MUHAMMAD ALI

b. 17 January 1942, 2, Louisville, Kentucky, USA
d. 03 June 2016, Scottsdale, Arizona, USA

Best Known For:

Being a boxing legend, his outspokenness on racism, his faith, conscientious objection to the Vietnam war, being a popular and inspirational icon to millions worldwide. Ali was born as Cassius Clay, he changed his name after converting to Islam, famously calling Clay his "slave name". He started boxing when he was 12. By the age of 22 he had won the world heavyweight championship, having turned professional in 1960 when he won the gold medal at the Rome Olympics (aged only 18). Of his 61 fights he was defeated only 5 times. He was the first to win the title Heavyweight Champion of the World three times, and remains the world record holder for this - a record he now shares with Lennox Lewis and Evander Holyfield. The first regain of his title was the infamous "Rumble in the Jungle" fight against George Foreman. This fight marked his return to boxing having been stripped of his title and unable to fight professionally following his conviction for refusing to enlist in the US Army for the Vietnam war - a conviction later overturned by the US Supreme Court. During the enforced break from boxing he became strongly involved in the Civil Rights movement, and was mentored by Malcolm X and Jesse Jackson, who did not share their contemporary Martin Luther King Jr's reputation for nonviolent change. Ali himself remained a committed peacemaker, and as one of the wealthiest sportsmen of his generation became a dedicated philanthropist helping those less fortunate than himself. Ali was diagnosed with Parkinson's in 1984 and used his position and reputation to raise awareness of the condition and created a research institute. This was not his only later life legacy however, and he continued to campaign against poverty and racism his entire life, in 2000 he hand delivered the poor nation economic debt wipe out petition to the UN having gained over 24M signatures from over 150 countries.

"A man who views the world the same at 50 as he did at 20 has wasted 30 years of his life"

"Hating people because of their color is wrong. And it doesn't matter which color does the hating. It's just plain wrong"

"*Thank you* is the best prayer that anyone could say. I say that one a lot. Thank you expresses extreme gratitude, humility, understanding"

ALICE WALKER

b. 09 February 1944, Putnam County, Georgia, USA

Best Known For:

The Colour Purple. Winner of a Pulitzer Prize, made into both film and musical it is considered one of the US' great contributions to literature. It is frequently studied in English speaking schools and colleges worldwide and credited with breaking many taboos, both in the nature of its first person dialogue that Walker herself calls "folk speech" and its subject matter. It has been both loved and loathed in equal measure for it's no holds barred depictions of racism, sexism and violence in 1930s America. Walker herself has been an outspoken campaigner for sex and racial equality, and some of her more staunchly held views - she is famously pro Palestine and refused to allow her works to be published in Israel, was arrested aged 59 at a war rally in Washington DC, supports David Icke's conspiracy theories about world leadership - have led her into frequent controversy.

"We don't see things as they are, we see them as we are"

ANAIS NIN

b. 21 February 1903, Neuilly-sur-Seine, France
d. 14 January 1977, Los Angeles, California, USA

Best Known For:

Her journals, bringing written erotica into the mainstream and feminist exploration of sexuality and morality creating an almost cult like status amongst her supporters. She wrote constantly from her teens until her death from cervical cancer. Her work consisted of both of her own thoughts and feelings, of philosophy, of psychology and of fiction. Eight volumes of her diaries have been published. As a both an artist and psychoanalyst herself she was fascinated by surrealism and much of her work has been adopted into that movement's bibliography. Her list of lovers reads like a who's who of the artistic and intellectual world at the time and included writers Henry Miller, Gore Vidal, John Steinbeck and the Austrian psychiatrist Otto Rank. Born to Cuban parents Nin lived between France and the United States. Long before it was popular to do so she self published her work for nearly 3 decades before it began to win acclaim in the 1960s.

"Until you make the unconscious conscious it will direct your life and you will call it fate"

CARL JUNG

b. 26 July, 1875, Kesswil, Thurgau, Switzerland
d. 06 June 1961, Kusnacht, Zurich, Switzerland

Best Known For:

Being the man for analytical psychology, his work on archetypes and collective unconscious, and still taking part in a pretty constant battle for title of the world's best shrink: was it Jung or Freud? Jung's early life was shaped by the family's poverty and his mother's depression and frequent periods of absence for ill health. As a child he was academically bright but did not enjoy school and often invented excuses to not attend. One of his coping mechanisms for dealing with his mother's absence was the creation of a small carving which he added to on a regular basis - when he discovered its similarity to some Australian Aboriginal practices he could not have known anything about, his ideas about collective unconscious were born. It was these, and the more spiritual side of his work that lead to his split from Freud. The two had worked together for nearly six years, Freud at the outset being terribly excited by the discovery of this protege who could continue his then fledgling work into psychoanalysis. They two parted company and in doing so two very different branches of analytical psychology and psychiatry were created.

"Do not dwell in the past, do not dream of the future, concentrate the mind on the present moment"

GAUTAMA BUDDHA

b. circa 563/480 BC, Lumbini, Nepal
d. Circa 483/400 BC, Kushinagar, India

Best Known For:

Founding Buddhism and being the one we most frequently call just "Buddha" - although the term is a Hindu word describing someone who has achieved enlightenment and is therefore technically open to be applied to anyone else who has. Nonetheless Buddha as we know him, Gautama Buddha or under his birth name of Siddhārtha Gautama is considered by most Hindus to be the ninth avatar of Vishnu, the god of preservation who incarnates himself in order to restore balance and wisdom to the planet. Although specific dates are debated without conclusion by historians what we do know is that Buddha was born in what is modern day Nepal, travelled the area extensively, was not excessively spiritual until he was nearly 30, became a beggar and practised asceticism as was the perceived method of enlightenment of the time and when that didn't work vowed to sit under a tree until it did. 49 days of meditation later at the age of 35 Buddha was born, giving the world "the middle way" and eightfold path as expressed and found in the Dhammapada.

"For beautiful eyes, look for the good in others; for beautiful lips, speak only words of kindness; and for poise, walk with the knowledge that you are never alone"

AUDREY HEPBURN

b. 4 May 1929, Ixelles, Belgium
D. 20 January 1993, Tolochenaz, Switzerland

Best Known For:

Breakfast at Tiffany's, being a style icon, her elegance and grace, an unusual accent and her humanitarian work. Hepburn had a uniquely European heritage, a British citizen she was born in Belgium, her part Austrian father was a divorced from a Dutch heiress when he married Hepburn's mother, a Dutch Baroness, who herself was also divorced from a Dutch oil baron of the East Indies - a marriage which gave Hepburn two elder half brothers. Initially supporters of Fascist movements her parents moved between London, Belgium and The Netherlands, until upon finding themselves in Arnheim when the Nazis occupation occured - and then the family was involved in the resistance movement. Near starvation and her brother's imprisonment gave Hepburn her lifelong dedication to UNICEF and humanitarian issues.

"Out of suffering have emerged the strongest souls; the most massive characters are seared with scars"

KHALIL GIBRAN

b. 6 January 1883, Bsharri, Lebanon
d. 10 April 1931, Saint Vincent's Catholic Medical Center, New York, USA

Best Known For:

Poetry, art and his iconic book *The Prophet* - which has gained literary cult status at certain points in 20th Century history, and again more recently in the 21st as his quotes and sayings appear on social media. Almost unbelievably, as his name is not so familiar, he is the third biggest selling poet after Shakespeare and Lao Tzu. Allegedly he considered himself an artist first and poetic philosopher second. Born in the Ottoman Empire in what is now Lebanon Gibran's mother moved him and his siblings to the US where he was schooled. He returned to the Middle East and Europe as a young man, training to be an artist in Paris and had many successful gallery exhibits of his whimsical drawings and paintings over his lifetime. His portfolio of portraits give great insight, those of his "friends" for example include the Swiss psychiatrist Carl Jung, Irish poet WB Yeats and "the daddy" of modern sculpture, Frenchman Auguste Rodin. Works are on display the world over, and there are museums in Bhassri and Beirut.

"The secret of genius is to carry the spirit of the child into old age, which means never losing your enthusiasm"

ALDOUS HUXLEY

b.26 July 1894, Godalming, Surrey, UK
d. 22 November 1963, Los Angeles County, California, USA

Best Known For:

Brave New World - his futuristic novel written in 1931 that foretold of a dystopian "World State". Set in what would be 2450, much of what was considered then to be scientific fantasy in areas such as genetic modification, controlled reproduction, drug dependency and subliminal manipulation are accepted today. From a middle class family in Surrey, Hubbard's childhood was not without difficulty as he lost his mother at the age of 14 and went blind for several years - a circumstance that kept him away from his first chosen field of medicine and left him with literature instead. A graduate of Oxford he taught briefly, and in a strange twist of fate the other great British dystopian writer, George Orwell (1984) was in his class. Concentrating more and more on his writing he became part of the Bloomsbury set that included D H Lawrence, Virginia Woolf, E. M. Forster and Bertrand Russell. Huxley wrote over 50 works of fiction and non-fiction, being nominated but never winning the Nobel Prize for literature 7 times. He moved to the United States in his early 40s but never became a US citizen.

"No act of kindness, no matter how small, is ever wasted"

AESOP

b. No one knows
d. No one knows
(But if he was real he was probably alive around 600 BC)

Best Known For:

Aesop's Fables. Aesop's Fables are a collection of stories and myths that were first written down around 300 BC but attributed to a slave who was freed because he was so intelligent that he became a guide and wise counsel to his masters. Considered to be moral anecdotes and parables, they are tales that are simple to tell but hold a deeper meaning. There are 725 stories in the compendium of Aesop's Fables, and include titles such as The Frightened Hares, The Boy Who Cried Wolf, The Astronomer Who Fell Into A Well and The Wolf in Sheep's Clothing.

"The seven social sins are:
Wealth without work
Pleasure without conscience
Knowledge without character
Commerce without morality
Science without humanity
Worship without sacrifice
Politics without principle"

FREDERICK LEWIS DONALDSON

b.10 September 1860, Ladywood, Birmingham, UK
d. 7 October 1953, Westminster, London, UK

Best Known For:

Being Archdeacon of Westminster from 1937 to 1946. A famously left-wing Anglican priest, Donaldson was well-known for his clarity of word, "fine speaking voice" and involvement in socialist change as well as his work for the Abbey itself.

"Humility is nothing but truth, and pride is nothing but lying"

ST VINCENT DE PAUL

b. 24 April 1581, Saint-Vincent-de-Paul, Landes, France
d. 27 September 1660, Paris, France

Best Known For:

Being the patron saint of horses and tireless work for the poor. He founded the Congregation of the Mission in 1624 - which still has nearly 3,000 priests in its ranks today - and the Daughters of Charity of Saint Vincent de Paul, which has nearly 20,000 nuns. In France the latter were known as the "grey nuns" because of the colour of their habit, although it's probably closer to blue than grey. Deeply sadly the Daughters have been hit with systematic abuse scandals dating back to the 1960s, 70s and 80s in France and the UK, particularly Scotland.

De Paul was made a saint in 1737, and became the patron saint of horses due to the story of his selling his horse to try to escape slavery. It did not work and he was imprisoned for probably two years in what is today Turkey around 1605. He had already graduated as a bachelor of Theology from Toulouse University at this time, and his capture and subsequent release only served to further his commitment to service of God and others.

"Down through the ages, there has always been the spiritual path. It's been passed on - it always will be - and if anybody ever wants it in any age, it's always there"

GEORGE HARRISON

b. 25 February 1943, Liverpool, UK
d. 29 November 2001, Los Angeles, California, USA

Best Known For:

Being one quarter of The Beatles. The Beatles are the largest band of musicians the world has ever produced - album sales stand at over 800M. With Paul McCartney and John Lennon, Harrison was always a member of The Beatles, their ultimate drummer Ringo Starr joined in 1962. Lennon and Harrison attended the same primary school, Dovedale, however Lennon was 3 years older and Harrison's position in the band was actually brought about through McCartney - who used to share the bus with Harrison to their senior school, Liverpool Institute High School for Boys. Rolling Stone magazine ranks Harrison as 11th greatest guitarist of all time in its last updated 2011 list. Awarded an MBE in 1965 with the other Beatles he allegedly turned down the OBE in 2000 as McCartney had already been knighted. Known as "the quiet one" Harrison was deeply spiritual and practised Hinduism.

"I used to be indecisive but now I am not quite sure"

TOMMY COOPER

b. 19 March 1921, Caerphilly, Glamorgan, UK
d. 15 April 1984, Her Majesty's Theatre, London, UK

Best Known For:

Sexist, inappropriate, stupidly daft British comedy and magic. Oh, and a Fez. Cooper was a much loved and ever present comedic influence on stage and television for nearly 40 years. Having circuited his native Wales with magic tricks and comedy since his teens, his big break came on BBC's talent show "New to You" in 1948. After that he became a pretty ever present force on British television, his slapstick comedy routines and innuendo-laden one liners made him not just a UK but a worldwide personality. He cited his influences as the legendary Laurel and Hardy for their situational hilarity and Bob Hope and Max Miller for stand-up. A heavy drinker his whole life Cooper's performances declined after a forgetful incident on Michael Parkinson's TV show where he did not check the safety catch of his guillotine for a magic trick - the quick thinking of the crew prevented an on-screen calamity. A real life on-screen calamity awaited however, and he died live on national television during a performance for ITV's London Weekend Television. The television broadcast went on uninterrupted and in footage the audience are seen laughing believing Cooper's collapse to be part of his act, but Cooper was pronounced dead on arrival at Westminster hospital close by.

"I can calculate the motion of heavenly bodies, but not the madness of people"

ISAAC NEWTON

b. 4 January 1643, Woolsthorpe, Lincolnshire, UK
d. 31 March 1727, Kensington, London, UK

Best Known For:

Modern calculus, building the first reflecting telescope, providing the mathematical theory for the speed of sound, cooling physics, laws of motion, trajectories of the planets, light frequencies and separation of particles, classical mechanics. His most famous discovery however comes from the almost mythical status story of the young man and the apple tree. In 1666 at the age of 23, at his family's home of Woolsthorpe Manor near Grantham, Newton, already a fellow under scholarship at Cambridge studying natural philosophy, watched an apple fall to the ground. He was home on a break from studies as most of the country had been effectively "shut down" to try and limit the spread of the last recorded incident of bubonic plague which killed around 200,000 that year. Much of Newton's most groundbreaking work was undertaken at Woolsthorpe. Natural philosophy was based largely in a style of musings and observation from ancient Greek wisdom that Newton's work in mathematic and physics generated a significant cultural departure from. The quote is something he allegedly muttered after losing a small fortune in the South Sea trading company!

"Now I am become Death, the destroyer of worlds"

ROBERT J OPPENHEIMER

b. 22 April 1904, New York City, New York, USA
d. 18 February 1967, Princeton, New Jersey, USA

Best Known For:

The atomic bomb. Oppenheimer was one of the leading scientists of the Manhattan Project, the US led initiative to produce a nuclear bomb during World War II. After pushing the button on the first nuclear test of the weapon in 1944, in his own words Oppenheimer said, "I remembered the line from the Hindu scripture, the Bhagavad-Gita; Vishnu is trying to persuade the Prince that he should **do** his duty and, to impress him, takes on his multi-armed form and says, *Now I am become Death, the destroyer of worlds*. I suppose we all thought that, one way or another". The USA dropped two atomic bombs on Japan, one at Hiroshima 06 August 1945 and one at Nagasaki 09 August 1945 killing 80,000 people instantly and probably between 200-250,000 in the following months and years. Oppenheimer spent some years working in nuclear energy following the end of WWII. During the late 1950s he became an outspoken campaigner for limiting the development and use of nuclear weapons and alongside Albert Einstein and Bertrand Russell was part of forming the humanitarian group World Academy of Art and Science in 1960.

"You can fool all the people some of the time, and some of the people all the time, but you cannot fool all the people all the time"

ABRAHAM LINCOLN

b. 12 February 1809, Hodgenville, Kentucky, USA
d. 15 April 1865, Washington D.C., USA

Best Known For:

Abolishing slavery, the Gettysburg Address and being the first US president to be assassinated (the second was James Garfield in 1881, William McKinley in 1901, and John F Kennedy who was shot and killed immediately in 1963). Lincoln, a Republican, was not his party's first choice and faced particular dissent from Southern states where slavery was rife. Undeterred however Lincoln, with his country in the middle of civil war, delivered a speech at Gettysburg that stands today as one of the most famous in western history for equal rights and democracy. He managed to banish slavery with a constitutional amendment and defeat the southern Confederate states, but was assassinated only 5 days after their surrender.

"Nothing is either good or bad only thinking makes it so"

WILLIAM SHAKESPEARE

b. 26 April 1564, Stratford-upon-Avon, UK
d. Stratford-upon-Avon, UK

Best Known For:

Being the greatest poet and playwright the world has produced. He still is the highest selling writer in the world, with estimates of around 4 billion copies of his works sold. He wrote 37 plays in his lifetime, including comedies, romance and historical recountings. They include Romeo and Juliet, Hamlet, Othello, The Merchant of Venice, King Lear, Macbeth, Henry V and Richard III. His plays are frequently studied not just in English speaking nations, nor purely by students of English Literature, but in translations by children and scholars the world over for their dramatic intent and effect, and the deep resonance each story creates through its depictions of the trials and tribulations of being human. Shakespeare performed for both Queen Elizabeth I and her successor King James I and his plays were successful enough in his lifetime to buy his own house and land - the second largest plot in his hometown of Stratford-Upon-Avon, Warwickshire. The Royal Shakespeare company still performs around the world today, in 1997 a reconstructed Globe Theatre - a copy of the original on the banks of the Thames were where many of Shakespeare's plays were introduced - was opened.

"To live is the rarest thing in the world. Most people exist, that is all"

OSCAR WILDE

b. 16 October 1854, Dublin, Ireland
d. 30 November 1900, Paris, France

Best Known For:

Being one of the world's other greatest poets and playwrights, and the original "Dandy". Wilde's wit, intelligence, flamboyance, bisexuality and laissez faire attitude toward pretty much everything except himself earned him notoriety, respect and scorn in equal measure. Born Oscar Fingal O'Flahertie Wills Wilde he was highly academic studying first in Dublin and then Oxford. Between 1879 and 1894 he wrote 9 plays including The Importance of Being Earnest and An Ideal Husband. His works gained him fast popularity, mainly because they were incredibly funny yet always with an almost machiavellian undertone which was the zeitgeist of the Victorian era. His one and only novel, The Picture of Dorian Gray was published in 1890 was considered completely immoral at the time. He was renowned for his outrageous styling and clothes, and became a strong proponent and founder of aestheticism, the philosophical movement more concerned with how things look than what their meaning or purpose might be (not to be confused with asceticism, the spiritual practice of lack, humility and poverty!). Wilde was imprisoned for homosexulaity following his affair with Lord Alfred Douglas. His last works De Profundis and The Ballad of Reading

Gaol reflected his experiences with a humility not expected by his previous devil-may-care attitude. He died in Paris of ill health and penniless.

"I have nothing to declare except my genius"

"The only difference between a saint and a sinner is that every sinner has a past and every sinner has a future"

"We are all in the gutter, but some of us are looking at the stars"

"The truth is rarely pure and never simple"

"Do not let the behavior of others destroy your inner peace"

DALAI LAMA XIV

b. 22 February 1940, Takster, Tibet

Best Known For:

Being the spiritual leader of the displaced Tibetan Buddhist people. The term Dalai Lama means Ocean of Wisdom and is one conferred on someone who has been identified by the High Lamas of Tibet as the reincarnation of the previous Lama. The Dalai Lama is one who has decided to become a tulku - that is someone who returns to the material planet to continue their work rather than moving on to afterlife. The current Dalai Lama is Tenzin Gyatso, shortened from Jetsun Jamphel Ngawang Lobsang Yeshe Tenzin Gyatso. He was born Lhamo Thondup, 6 July 1935 in Takster, Tibet and identified when he was two. He is the 14th Dalai Lama. The Chinese removed Tibetan self rule the same year that Gyatso was appointed its leader. Following the Tibetan Uprising in 1959 he fled his homeland and has lived in exile since. He was awarded the Nobel Peace Prize in 1989 for his continual drive for peaceful return of Tibet to the Tibetan people. He currently lives Mcleod Ganj, India and has 18.8M followers on twitter.

"Being deeply loved by someone gives you strength, while loving someone deeply gives you courage"

LAO TZU

b. No one knows, Chu, China, probably
d. 553 BC, maybe, Zhou, China

Best Known For:

Being the author of the Tao Te Ching, allegedly, and founder of Taoism. Also known as Laozi or Lao-Tze he is the second best selling poet of all time after William Shakespeare. Much of his history is unknown, indeed historians are unable to agree as to whether he was alive in the 4th or 6th Centuries BC. The Tao Te Ching is a book of verse and prose that seeks to identify the origins of the universe and man's role within it. As such it has influenced many thinkers over the years, most notably in modern psychology Carl Jung and his theories on the collective unconscious. The Tao Te CHing focuses on connection with the Tao, or Dao - the flow of divine energy which manages and manifest all things across the cosmos. Including people. When practising this way of life followers are held in this natural and powerful flow and are in complete harmony with all.

"A hero is someone who understands the responsibility that comes with his freedom"

BOB DYLAN

b. 24 May 1941, Duluth, Minnesota, USA

Best Known For:

Cult status as a singer-songwriter due to the political and philosophical nature of his lyrics. Ostensibly a folk singer he is famed for switching instruments, styles and genres and is still performing today at the age of 77 on his "never ending tour" which began in 1988. At the time of writing (November 2018) he had just finished a European tour and was set to perform a number of dates in the US leading up to Christmas. His records have sold over 100 million copies and in 2016 he received the Nobel Prize for Literature for poetic expression in his song lyrics.

The actual number of songs he has penned is unconfirmed, however it is estimated between 4-5 hundred, and includes tracks such as Blowin in the Wind, Mr Tambourine Man and The Times They Are A-Changin'.

"Your time is limited, so don't waste it living someone else's life. Don't be trapped by dogma - which is living with the results of other people's thinking. Don't let the noise of others' opinions drown out your own inner voice. And most important, have the courage to follow your heart and intuition"

STEVE JOBS

b. 24 February 1955, San Francisco, California, USA
d. 5 October 2011, Palo Alto, California, USA

Best Known For:

Apple, the legendary battles with Microsoft and then Samsung and his own teams in order to create designs he felt surpassed anything else available. Credited with the rise of intuitive design Jobs was renowned as being incredibly inspirational and intensely difficult simultaneously. Fairly uneducated in a traditional sense he dropped out of college and toured India seeking enlightenment. There he studied zen buddhism and attempted to bring many of its principles into the culture of his business and design of his products. Apple Macs were in long held competition with the more clunky yet less monopolistic microsoft computers for many years, but with the release of the first iPhone 29 June 2007 Apple took over the market of handheld devices and its position has remained strong ever since. Touch screen multi functioning phones and iPads are the legacy of Jobs, and whilst many mimics have appeared he always maintained a commitment to style and function that is the hallmark of the Apple brand. Jobs died of breathing problems caused by his pancreatic cancer at the age of 56, at the time of his death Jobs's net worth was estimated at $10.2BN.

"You have to trust in something, your gut, destiny, life, karma, whatever"

"Believing that the dots will connect down the road will give you the confidence to follow your heart"

"Success is not final, failure is not fatal: it is the courage to continue that counts"

"Attitude is a little thing that makes a big difference"

"If you're going through hell, keep going"

WINSTON CHURCHILL

b. 30 November 1874, Woodstock, Oxfordshire, UK
d. 24 January 1965, Kensington, London, UK

Best Known For:

Being British Prime Minister in World War II, gathering his allies together to defeat Hitler, restoring the world order and powerful leadership. Churchill was Prime Minister twice, from 1940 to 1945 and 1951 to 1955. In a radio interview after his retirement Churchill remarked that as a child he'd always been convinced he would die young, so didn't really decide to try and make the most of his life until his forties, when he realised it wasn't going to happen. Churchill was first a soldier, serving in the Sudan and Boer Wars. He became a correspondent to the press in these times and so his life in public began. Whilst widely recognised for preventing Nazi rule in Europe and viewed as a hero he is also not seen as without controversy in some of his own decisions, and it is well documented that neither Chamberlain nor King George VI were very keen on his becoming Prime Minister during World War II. He was famed for his eloquent rhetoric, speeches and writing. He was nominated for the Nobel Peace Prize and won the Nobel Prize for Literature. Upon death he was given a State funeral, usually reserved for the monarchy.

"I may be drunk, Miss, but in the morning I will be sober and you will still be ugly"

"We make a living by what we get, but we make a life by what we give"

"Great minds discuss ideas; average minds discuss events; small minds discuss people"

ELEANOR ROOSEVELT

b. 11 October 1884, New York City, USA
d. 7 November 1962, New York City, USA

Best Known For:

Well it could be the longest serving First Lady of the USA thanks to President Franklin D. Roosevelt, but actually it's more a prolific contribution to human rights. She spent seven years as US Delegate to the United Nations from 1945 to 1952 and was a committed member for the United Nations Commision on Human Rights. Roosevelt was the first First Lady to really make the role a position of influence in her own right, possibly aided by her husband's lack of mobility. She frequently stood on his behalf, took her own tours, held her own press conferences and was outspoken on race and women's issues.

"It is not fair to ask of others what you are not willing to do yourself"

"There is no passion to be found playing small - in settling for a life that is less than the one you are capable of living"

NELSON MANDELA

b. 18 July 1918, Mvezo, South Africa
d. 5 December 2013, Johannesburg, South Africa

Best Known For:

Ending Apartheid in South Africa, after being imprisoned for 27 years. On his release Mandela smiled, waved and got directly to work with FW de Klerk, leader of the party that imprisoned him, to end apartheid. Apartheid was a system of segregation not only of black and white but of different tribes of blacks designed to remove the power of the black majority and maintain that of the white minority. South African had born witness to disgraceful racism for many years, however at a time when the rest of the world was coming into peace after WWII and trying to improve civil rights and human equality South Africa introduced apartheid. At this time, 1948, Mandela was already involved in the African National Congress having founded its youth league in 1944. Originally committed to nonviolence the increasing rather than decreasing entrenchment of racism into South African law led to massive demonstrations and violence, including the planning of armed overthrow. Mandela, a qualified lawyer, was arrested and released several times, gradually losing any rights to work or travel.

In October 1963 Mandela was tried for sabotage under suppression of communism laws and found guilty along with 10 others. Even awaiting sentencing Mandela reiterated his desire to see a South Africa where all peoples regardless of race were treated equally and with respect, known as "the speech from the dock". There was increasing world pressure on FW De Klerk as Mandela's health failed under his by then house arrest (having served nearly 20 years on Robben Island and another 6 years at Pollsmoor). The ANC, with other prohibited parties, was unbanned 2 February 1990, and Mandela released 9 days later. He immediately took over leadership of the ANC and began negotiations with de Klerk. They were jointly awarded the Nobel Peace Prize in 1993 and 27 April 1994 saw South Africa's first free elections - the first time Mandela himself had the right to vote. He was elected president by a landslide and served until 1999. Following his retirement from politics he began the Nelson Mandela Foundation and began to work against poverty and AIDS, work he continued although more quietly after 2004 due to his health, until his death in 2013.

"For to be free is not merely to cast off one's chains, but to live in a way that respects and enhances the freedom of others"

"The cure for boredom is curiosity. There is no cure for curiosity"

DOROTHY PARKER

b. 22 August 1893, Long Branch, New Jersey, USA
D. 07 June 1967, New York City, New York, USA

Best Known For:

Being very witty, although apparently it annoyed her that this was the cornerstone of her reputation. It is unsurprising however, when challenged to come up with an amusing sentence with the word "horticulture" in it Parker famously responded, "well, you can lead a whore to culture but you can't make her think". A privileged yet abusive childhood leant Parker an air of aloofness which many have commented lead to her immediate recourse to humour. A critic, author and poet she wrote freelance for many sources and had a column in the New Yorker magazine in her early twenties before moving to Los Angeles to become a screenwriter. She was nominated for two Oscars for screenwriting, most notably for A Star is Born in 1937 which was one of the first feature films made in technicolour and starred Janet Gaynor and Fredric March. It has now been remade several times - in 1954 with Judy Garland, 1976 with Barbra Streisand and Kris Kristofferson and now in 2018 with Lady Gaga and Bradley Cooper.

"Very little is needed to make a happy life; it is all within yourself, in your way of thinking"

MARCUS AURELIUS

b. 26 April 121, Rome, Italy
d. 17 March 180, possibly in Austria but records are not agreed

Best Known For:

Being a very clever Roman Emperor. Aurelius reigned from 161 to 180. His death is often considered to be the turning point in the fall of the Roman Empire and certainly signalled the end of Pax Romana - the peaceful co-existence of countries which were attached or annexed to Rome from the time of Augustus in AD 31. Aurelius was a practitioner of Stoicism, the Greek philosophical school begun by Zeno based on a practice not dissimilar to that espoused in the Tao Te Ching - connection to and harmony with the divine source - although in the Stoics' case that source is considered to be reason. Stoics seeking this wisdom are therefore encouraged not to attach feelings to pleasure or pain - hence the modern usage of the word stoic to describe someone who endures circumstance without reaction or attachment. Aurelius' own writings, known as Meditations, are considered to be a profound expression of this philosophy and its practical application. They are still studied today both as academic and practical tests for students of psychology and philosophy.

"The more clearly we can focus our attention on the wonders and realities of the universe about us, the less taste we shall have for destruction"

RACHEL CARSON

b. 27 May 1907, Springdale, Pennsylvania, USA
D. 14 April 1964, Silver Spring, Maryland, USA

Best Known For:

Being a marine biologist and leading the field in environmental work and sustainability. Carson wrote with a love of nature throughout her life, pursuing her academic studies to culminate with a Masters in Zoology in 1932. During the 1940s and 50s she wrote frequently for radio broadcasts and magazines, articles such as "Help Your Child to Wonder" showing her altruistic intent throughout her career. Her books *The Sea Around Us* and *The Edge of the Sea* were the leading marine biology texts of the time. Until her death she campaigned for better sustainability, understanding and appreciation of the world's natural resources and the link between the health of the planet and that of human beings - long before it was popularly accepted. Her 1962 work *Silent Spring* is seen as a turning point for agricultural and marine farming practices. She was awarded the Presidential Medal of Freedom for her environmental foresight in 1980.

"Imagination is more important than knowledge. Knowledge is limited. Imagination encircles the world"

ALBERT EINSTEIN

b. 14 March 1879, Ulm, Germany
d. 18 April 1955, Princeton Medical Center, New Jersey, USA

Best Known For:

Science, the theory of relativity, $E = mc^2$, allegedly the world's most well known mathematical formula although how much of the world knows what it means is probably a different matter, and being the world's most celebrated and popular genius. On that note $E = mc^2$ is only one part of the theory of relativity - known as Special Relativity. It was the final equation of Einstein's "miracle year" 1905 research papers developed at Zurich University, papers that catapulted Einstein from a respected scientist in his field to the globally recognised thinker he became - aged just 26. Other principles he established in that year formed the basis of quantum mechanics as we understand it today. His special relativity theory explored mass and matter not as distinct entities but as related ones, where capacity for energy and movement rather than resting output was key. The only problem with $E = mc^2$ was that it did not allow for Newton's law of gravity, the famous apple falling from the tree inspired moment of 350 years previous. Einstein didn't think Newton was essentially "wrong" however - just that something was missing. He published the General Theory of Relativity 10 years later in 1915. In this he established that the special theory allowing for gravitation as first identified in Newtonian physics and movement at the speed of light regardless of the distance between objects could and did exist together on the basis of a curved relationship between space and time. These two theories on relativity, the special and the general, form the theory of relativity. Nearly every piece of work in the arena of astronomical, quantum, and space travel progress since has proceeded on the basis of this curved space-time continuum. Einstein not only produced scientific papers, many hundreds, but philosophical, cultural and sociological works too. Einstein was born in Germany, lived in Italy and Switzerland as a child, but was a national of no nation whatsoever due to the perpetually shifting landscape of the German Empire, Austro-Hungarian Empire and Prussia as a child. He died with joint Swiss and US citizenship having given up his German citizenship in 1933 during the rise of Hitler's Third Reich and Weimar's dissolution. Born Jewish he stayed in the USA at the outbreak of war. He joined with British philosopher Bertrand Russell et al to argue for preventative measures against pursuing some of the atomic and nuclear weapons made possible by his own theories. He received many awards including the Nobel Prize for Physics.

"The ideals which have lighted me on my way and time after time given me new courage to face life cheerfully, have been Truth, Goodness, and Beauty"

**The End,
of Volume I, anyway.**

ABOUT THE AUTHOR:

Heather Jane-James is an artist, consciousness coach and writer. She lives in West Sussex with her children and a few animals. She compiled this book after years of creating inspirational social media. Her thinking was that whilst it's very nice to have these quotes on devices, it might be even nicer to have some in a book with a bit more meaning. Her first non-fiction, a collection of essays on spiritual principles, "Musings and A Few Unchallengeable Truths" is available on Amazon. This is her second work. She has two books due out in 2019, "Through the Noise and What You'll Find There" and "Don't Believe Everything You Think", although she's now thinking there's a few more Brilliant Quote Volumes to come! Heather can be contacted through her website at www.heatherjanejames.com.

With thanks to my sources: the library, the internet and a good education.

33953648R00038

Printed in Poland
by Amazon Fulfillment
Poland Sp. z o.o., Wrocław